D0965846

American Indian Authors for Young Readers

A selected bibliography

Compiled and with an introduction by Mary Gloyne Byler

Association on American Indian Affairs: New York

The Association on American Indian Affairs (432 Park Avenue South, New York, N.Y. 10016) is a private non-profit, national citizens' organization supported by its members and contributors. It assists Indian and Alaska Native communities in their efforts to achieve full economic, social, and civil equality.

Library of Congress Catalog Card Number 73-82110.

Printed in the United States of America.

Photograph on cover by Ricco Montevecchi

FOREWORD

Well over six-hundred children's books were examined during a four-year period in the preparation of this bibliography. Roughly two out of three were rejected out-of-hand because the contents or illustrations were conspicuously offensive. A closer look at the remaining two-hundred-or-so books proved discouraging. The prevalence of more subtle stereotypes, misconceptions and clichés led to further rejections. Finally, it was decided to limit selection to American Indian authors.

While non-Indian authors may produce well-written and entertaining children's books featuring American Indians, there is little in their stories that tells us much about American Indians. We do learn what non-Indians imagine Indians to be, or think they should be.

There is more to being an American Indian—Apache, Seneca, Hopi, or whatever tribe—than can be acquired through an act of will, a course of study, or discovering an Indian ancestor somewhere in the family tree. It is not an intellectual choice. In short, being Indian is growing up Indian: it is a way of life, a way of thinking and being. Shaped by their own life experiences, non-Indians lack the feelings and insights essential to a valid representation of what it means to be an American Indian.

This bibliography is short. It is short because there are so few books for children written by American Indians. One reason for this is that publishers have had little interest in developing American Indian authors.

Additionally, the oral tradition by which American Indians convey and perpetuate vast bodies of knowledge does not contain a section of literature that is exclusively for children. This oral tradition, free from the limits imposed by the written word, does not tailor its material to appeal to varying age groups.

Those "quaint" fables, myths and "animal stories" that have been "adapted" for children often have many levels of meaning in the original versions—meanings that a child may grasp at the varying stages of his or her development and may come to fully understand only with the passage of time and an ever-growing experience of life.

This bibliography contains many books that would not ordinarily appear in a listing of books for children. But in the oral tradition, those who have information share it with those who do not. In this spirit then, it is up to those who can read to embrace the oral tradition and share what they read with those who cannot. At this point in time it is the only way very young children will be able to learn what American Indians are saying and writing about themselves.

MGB

Introduction

American Indians have had to struggle for more than their physical survival. It is not only land that has been appropriated; it has also been a fight to keep mind and soul together, for along with the United States Cavalry, missionaries, educators and the "Americanizers," have come the writers of books about Indians.

Down through the years the publishing industry has produced thousands of books about American Indians—a subject that fascinates many. Fact and fiction—it is not always possible to tell which is which—have rolled off the presses since "frontier" days. But American Indians in literature, today as in the past, are merely images projected by non-Indian writers.

Most minority groups in this country have been, and are still, largely ignored by the nation's major publishing houses—particularly in the field of children's books. American Indians, on the other hand, contend with a mass of material about themselves. If anything, there are too many children's books about American Indians.

There are too many books featuring painted, whooping, befeathered Indians closing in on too many forts, maliciously attacking "peaceful" settlers or simply leering menacingly from the background; too many books in which white benevolence is the only thing that saves the day for the incompetent, childlike Indian; too many stories setting forth what is "best" for American Indians.

There are too many stories for very young children about little boys running around in feathers and headbands, wearing fringed buckskin clothing, moccasins and (especially) carrying little bows and arrows. The majority of these books deal with the unidentified past. The characters are from unidentified tribes and they are often not even afforded the courtesy of personal names. In fact, the only thing identifiable is the stereotyped image of the befeathered Indian.

This depersonalization is common in books for children. In *Good Hunting Little Indian* (Young Scott Books) the characters are referred to as Little Indian, Mama Indian and Papa Indian, calling to mind Mama Bear, Papa Bear and Baby Bear. But, in *Granny and the Indians* (Macmillan) the same author personalizes the "Granny" by giving her a name (Granny Guntry) while the other characters are simply "the Indians"—who are made to look silly and ridiculous both in the story and in the illustrations. The pictures in both of the books contain a baffling hodgepodge of Indian dress.

The device of repeatedly referring to people in this impersonal and anonymous way, and then reinforcing the anonymity with illustrations that are nondescript, creates the impression that one is not dealing with full-fledged human beings.

Many books parody Indian life and customs, holding them up to ridicule and derision. *Indian Two Feet and his Eagle Feather* (Childrens Press) is about a little boy (Indian Two Feet) and how he earns the right to wear an eagle feather. This makes a mockery of those tribes that consider eagle feathers symbolic of courage and honor, and it equates the process of earning them with child's play.

A much-used theme is that of a child in search of his "real" name. According to the jacket copy on *Little Indian* (Simon & Schuster), readers will "gleefully" discover that there is more than one way to acquire a name. This story distorts and makes fun of the name-giving practices of some tribes and makes of them whimsical, meaningless exercises to be viewed with humor.

The degree to which a non-Indian author's concept of things "Indian" is distorted and an example of how distortions are kept alive are demonstrated in a book called *Buffalo Man and Golden Eagle* (McCall Publishing Co.).

The book begins with that quaint old "Indian" expression, "Many moons ago." Why not simply say "a long time ago"? According to the story, Golden Eagle (also referred to as "the Indian") hunted six days a week, but on the seventh day he would don "his most beautiful headdress, put his peace pipe in his mouth, and stroll off into the hills."

The six-day work week is misplaced in the context of time; it did not exist for American Indians. The tribes that wore headdresses wore them only on special occasions, not to "stroll" around in. Peace pipes were smoked ritually and in the proper ceremonial setting. So while Golden Eagle, or "the Indian," adheres to the biblical injunction against working on the Sabbath, he is disrespectful towards ceremonial and religious articles that are particularly American Indian—all in five lines of text with a total of seventy-five words.

This book was originally published in Austria. The author was born in Germany, studied in Munich, now lives in Bavaria and raises riding ponies. The story is designed to convey a lesson about cooperation and friendship. The real message, however, is that publishing houses in the United States will go to Europe for books about American Indians but are hesitant to venture into Indian country here at home.

It is one thing to write about imaginary beings from an imaginary time and place, but American Indians are real people and deserve the dignity of being presented as such. These little books with their "charming" stories, fanciful illustrations and cute little characters put Indians in the same category with witches, ogres, giants, fairies, and baby animals.

Some authors indulge in what amounts to acts of cultural vandalism. An example of this is in *Pink Puppy* (Putnam's). The setting is among the Cherokees in North Carolina.

The book opens with a wake for Cindy Standingdeer's mother. The author's understanding of a Cherokee wake and of the dynamics involved is highly superficial. Cindy, eight-years-old, feels that because people are singing they are happy. Since most Cherokee children are taken to wakes from the time they are infants, it is unlikely that an eight-year-old would so grossly misunderstand the hymn singing in this way.

The old "stoic Indian" cliché is thrown in when the author has Grandmother Standingdeer say to Cindy, "Cherokees don't cry. You'll have to learn the old Indian way—it's a good way." The school teacher (white) arrives and urges Cindy to cry, saying, "That's all right Cindy. Go ahead. You'll feel better." And later she adds, "I'll cry with you Cindy."

The author cannot have attended many Cherokee wakes or funerals or it would be obvious that Cherokees do indeed cry. However, if it were true that Cherokees do not cry, and if it is really the "old Indian way," then the teacher, in encouraging the child to cry, is interfering with behavioral and cultural patterns in a very direct way. She is undermining the grandmother's position and is saying, in effect, that the "old Indian way" is not a good way, after all.

Cindy is "glad her grandmother didn't come up close and put her arm around her the way the white people do." But, she accepts the embrace of the teacher, "a young white woman," without a qualm.

Cindy becomes abstracted and it is alleged that "somebody had a medicine man conjure her." It is irresponsible of the author to introduce the subject of witchcraft and medicine men. Responsible scholars hesitate to make judgments about the extent to which present-day Cherokees in western North Carolina believe in or practice conjuration.

Whatever the Cherokees think or feel about conjuration, a medicine man is a figure to be respected and should not be equated with a capricious wicked witch who casts spells on innocent children.

Cindy's father keeps her home from school "day after day" because he is lonely. He agrees to take his family (three children and himself) to live with his mother because her house is "bigger and it's better built."

A book of this sort is all the more insidious because it is well meant and is not obviously bad. The language itself is not derogatory. It is the impressions the words convey that are objectionable: the grandmother is a cold person untouched by the death of her daughter; the father is an industrious but incompetent and selfish man who cannot provide his family with adequate shelter.

The teacher is the only person who comforts or sympathizes with Cindy. She is warm, understanding and concerned.

The book is supposedly about a young Cherokee girl, but it is really about the pretty young white teacher who copes with the problems created by the death of the girl's mother. The implication is that it is the non-Indian only who can solve problems and make decisions for American Indians because Indians are not capable of doing so.

This patronizing attitude is indicative of an arrogance that sometimes borders on the grotesque. In *Trading Post Girl* (Frederick Fell, Inc.), the following passage occurs: "Libby gave Barney a teasing glance. 'Red earth, white clouds and blue water—Daddy, are you patriotic!'

'Well, now, Punkin, I guess you're right. This really is a piece of our American life, right among the Indians. You wait and see, some day they'll be real fine American citizens.'

'Oh, Daddy, not those savages.'

'They've got a lot of things to learn, too, honey. Give them time. They've got lots of good in them.' "

The author, under the guise of fairness, is telling us that American Indians are not "patriotic," are not "real fine" citizens, and that they have "lots of good in them" in spite of the fact that they are "savages."

A number of authors have taken it upon themselves to establish the humanity of American Indians by presenting arguments for and against the idea. Humanness is not an arguable point.

One of the factors that significantly contributes to and nourishes this kind of arrogance is the way American Indians are portrayed in history books. This description of "the Indian" appears in *The French and Indian Wars* (American Heritage Junior Library): "To the Indians pity was a form of cowardice. Their captives were no longer persons but things to be exchanged for ransom or tortured for amusement according to their shifting savage moods. The custom of scalping was symbolic of the Indian mind, a mind so apart from that of the whites as to remain incomprehensible. So heedless were the red men of human suffering that the word cruelty seems inadequate to describe their ingenious tortures. Even the gentle Roger Williams called them 'wolves with the brains of men.' "

This description is in sharp contrast to the following statements from Hodge's scholarly *Handbook of Indians North of Mexico:* "From the days of Columbus to the present travelers have given testimony of customs and manners of Indians . . . which displayed a regard for the happiness and well being of others." "Abundant evidence might be adduced to show that Indians are often actuated by motives of pure benevolence and do good merely from a generous delight in the act." "Truth, honesty, and the safeguarding of human life were everywhere recognized as essential to the peace and prosperity of a tribe, and social customs enforced their observance." "The care of one's family was regarded as a social duty and was generally observed." "Honesty was inculcated in the young and exacted in the tribe."

Non-Indian writers have created an image of American Indians that is almost sheer fantasy. It is an image that is not authentic and one that has little value except that of sustaining the illusion that the original inhabitants deserved to lose their land because they were so barbaric and uncivilized.

This fantasy does not take into account the rich diversity of cultures that did, and do, exist. Violence is glorified over gentleness and love of peace. The humanistic aspects of American Indian societies are ignored in the standard book.

A book of "Indian stories" for young readers published in the 1930s proclaimed itself a "fine collection of exciting stories in which Indian war whoops fairly echo through the pages and painted savages peek out behind each word."

The world has changed a lot since then, but the publishing industry has not. In 1968 Harper & Row published *Indian Summer,* an "I CAN READ History Book" for children ages four through eight. According to the jacket copy it is "wonderful—geared to that important group, late first through third grade. . . . It is a perfect book."

The setting for the story is a log cabin in a Kentucky forest during the time when the American colonies were fighting to gain independence from Britain. While the man of the house is away fighting with the American forces, men of some unidentified tribe skulk around the cabin. The "pioneer" woman outwits them and they retreat hastily into the forest. The author in a fit of incredible cuteness has contrived to work the sound "ugh" into the story.

The message a child gets from this "history" book is that the settlers are good, peaceful people who love their homes and families, and that American Indians are menacing but stupid creatures called "redskins" who can be made fools of by a lone woman. The "pioneer" woman is bravely and courageously defending her home and children. The father is patriotic and dutiful. There is nothing in *Indian Summer* indicating that American Indians are also fathers and mothers with families and homes.

Undoubtedly it is accurate that settlers were threatend by, and afraid of, Indians, but Indians were equally, if not more, threatened by the settlers and they had much more to lose. The history books and story books seldom make it clear that Native Americans in fighting back, were defending their homes and families and were not just being malicious.

It is rarely, if ever, mentioned that non-Indians scalped people, but scalping as an Indian practice is emphasized in most of the books about American Indians, including the textbooks used in schools throughout the country.

For example, in *Indian Summer* these statements occur: "Those Indians are after your scalps." "Then they could have scalped you a long way from the cabin. That's an old Indian trick." A book called *Tough Enough's Indians* (Walck, Inc.) has this to say, " 'Injuns didn't go fussin' up their critters that-a-way.' Beanie said.

'They didn't have time. They were too busy huntin' and fishin' and beatin' drums and scalpin' other Injuns and white folks, cuttin' their skin and hair right off, somethin' terrible, and burnin 'em up at stakes.' " *Pontiac, King of the Great Lakes* (Hastings House) contains this sentence, "A warrior had only to drop his canoe into the water and he was on his way to a council, a feast, or some scalp-taking expedition of his own."

The frequency with which non-Indian authors mention scalping, and the relish with which they indulge in bloody descriptions, would indicate that it is they, rather than Indians, who are preoccupied with scalps.

Contrary to what people have been led to believe, scalping was not a wide-spread custom among American Indian tribes. Scalping was practiced by the ancient Scythians as long ago as the fifth century B.C., but research shows that it was not a very old practice on the American continent, and was originally confined to an area limited to the eastern United States and the lower St. Lawrence region, excluding New England and much of the Atlantic Coast region.

According to the *Handbook of American Indians North of Mexico,* compiled in the late 1800s, "The numerous popular misconceptions in connection with the scalping practice may be recapitulated in a series of negatives. The custom was not general, and in most regions where found was not even ancient. The trophy did not include any part of the skull or even the whole scalp. The operation was not fatal. The scalp was not always evidence of the killing of an enemy, but was sometimes taken from a victim who was allowed to live. It was not always taken by the same warrior who had killed or wounded the victim. It was not always preserved by the victor. The warrior's honors were not measured by the number of his scalps."

The *Handbook* further states, "The spread of the scalping practice over a great part of central and western United States was a direct result of the encouragement in the shape of scalp bounties offered by the colonial and more recent governments. . . ."

The Puritans offered rewards for Indian heads. As early as 1641 New Amsterdam (New York City) paid bounties for Indian scalps, as did other colonies.

In 1755, Massachusetts paid £40 (about $200) for the scalp of an adult male Indian and £20 (about $100) for the scalps of women and children. The French and English, in addition to paying for Indian scalps, offered rewards for the scalps of white people. Many non-Indians took advantage of the opportunity to supplement the family income by collecting scalp bounties.

There were many tribes who never took scalps. In all fairness, a more balanced approach is needed. In 1972, in an obvious attempt to counteract such books as *Indian Summer, Tough Enough's Indians,* and *Pontiac,* Harper & Row brought out a book entitled *Small Wolf* in which Small Wolf, a young boy from an unidentified tribe, goes hunting on what is now Manhattan Island. He sees many strange sights including a man whose face is "all WHITE." He brings his father to the island and they are run off at gunpoint by an irate Dutchman. The settlers grow in numbers, occupying more and more land, repeatedly forcing Small Wolf and his family to pack their belongings and move.

While it is admirable that Harper & Row is willing to attempt to present an Indian point of view, the book is not without flaws. The man whose face is "all WHITE" is described as having "a fat jaw and cracks between his teeth," so that Small Wolf thinks he is wearing a "devil mask." The illustration shows a fat, ugly, leering man (Dutch). The implication is that "bad" people are physically unattractive—not to be confused with good, clean-cut Americans.

Historically the "devil mask" is misplaced; the devil is a Judeo-Christian concept, not an American Indian one.

This book fosters a common misunderstanding about American Indians and the concept of land ownership. "They [other Indians] had no right to sell the land. The land and the sky and the sea are all Mother Earth for everyone to use," says Small Wolf's father.

This bit of dialogue presents a simplistic and highly romanticized version of what were various practical concepts of land ownership. It leaves the impression that American Indians had *no* concept of land ownership at all.

The Native peoples of this country were not rootless wanderers drifting about the country helter skelter. Certainly, when the colonists landed, the people who owned the land did not have deeds and fee-simple titles to whip out and exhibit as proof of ownership; however the various tribes and bands did claim sovereignty over specific areas of land, dwelling, hunting, and farming within well-established boundaries.

The people who came here to establish colonies were, after all, in search of a piece of land to own. Historically and philosophically one rationalization for the seizure of Indian-owned lands is that nobody owned the land anyhow. Much book space has been, and is being, devoted to maintaining that myth. Apparently the producers of books feel that the American public and system of government can not stand the truth.

The ending of *Small Wolf* gives the impression that American Indians eventually just faded into the sunset. This denies the fact that there are American Indians around today.

While non-Indians are portrayed negatively, they ultimately come across as being strong and aggressive. Small Wolf and his family evoke a feeling of pity. American Indians want respect, not pity—it is demeaning and denies human dignity.

This book is a sincere effort to offset the negative images portrayed in books like *Indian Summer*. But both of these books exemplify a flaw common to most books about Indians: they are portrayed either as noble superhumans, or as depraved, barbarous subhumans. There is no opportunity for them to behave like mere human beings.

A more direct assault is made upon the humanity of American Indians by the use of key words and phrases which trigger negative and derogatory images. Words such as savage, buck, squaw and papoose do not bring to mind the same images as do the words man, boy, woman and baby.

Descriptions of half-naked, hideously-painted creatures brandishing tomahawks or scalping knives, yelping, howling, grunting, jabbering, or snarling are hardly conducive to a sympathetic reaction to the people so described. Ethnocentric bias is translated into absurdities, i.e. making a point of the fact that American Indians could not read or write English when the Pilgrims arrived; they did not have clocks; they had no schools.

Broad generalizations are made, obliterating individuality. Such generalizations, while convenient, serve to foster and sustain stereotypic misconceptions. For example, in *The Indians of the Plains* (American Heritage Junior Library) this pronouncement occurs, "War was the Indian's career and hobby, his work and his play."

The author does not mention that some tribes considered warfare to be an expression of insanity. Others strove to maintain peace and harmony in all phases of their existence. Besides, it is doubtful that there was actually much inter-tribal "war" before the coming of the white men.

Extensive cultural bias is evidenced by the comparisons invited by authors in their descriptions of people. In *Something for the Medicine Man* (Melmont), the "Granny," a Cherokee woman, is described as having a face that is "dried up like a persimmon." The teacher (non-Indian) is "tall as the trees," not "old like Granny," and has eyes "like blue flags"—the baby (Cherokee) has eyes "like a baby fox." The Cherokee family eats "like hungry dogs."

The non-Indian teacher in *My Name is Lion* (Holiday House) is young, and smells "like too many flowers." A Navajo lady is described as "an old woman" who is sitting "huddled in a blanket." Lion, a Navajo boy who finds he does not "mind" the way the teacher smells, discovers that the Navajo woman "sure" does not smell "like that flower teacher." Lion's grandfather is drunk, dirty, and "whining in Navajo about money." The positive intent of both of these books is canceled by the negative aspects of the implied comparisons.

The repeated juxtaposition of man and animal serves to instill and reinforce the image of American Indians as being not only subhuman but also inhuman beings. In *Captives of the Senecas* (Hale & Co.), Senecas are described, "A ring of painted Indians was closing in on them, darting like huge weasles through the grass of the intervale." A later sentence reads, "Indians were coursing the ground like hunting dogs." *The American Indian* (Random House) has this to say, "The Indians hung around New Amsterdam, as the colony on Manhattan Island was called, and made themselves a nuisance. They were lazy, insolent, and thievish as monkeys." *The French and Indian Wars* (American Heritage Junior Library) puts forth this thought, "The Indian might turn gentle, but as with a tame wolf, it was a gentleness never to be trusted." *The Secret Name* (Harcourt Brace) has this statement, "Dad thinks Indians are like wild animals. . . . You can tame them a little bit, but not all the way."

It has been well established by sociologists and psychologists that the effect on children of negative stereotypes and derogatory images is to engender and perpetuate undemocratic and unhealthy attitudes that will plague our society for years to come.

It is time for American publishing houses, schools, and libraries to take another look at the books they are offering children and seriously set out to offset some of the damage they have done. Only American Indians can tell non-Indians what it is to be Indian. There is no longer any need for non-Indian writers to "interpret" American Indians for the American public.

Mary Gloyne Byler

PUBLISHER'S NOTE: *Mary Gloyne Byler is an enrolled member of the Eastern Band of Cherokee Indians of North Carolina and editor of* Indian Affairs, *the newsletter of the Association on American Indian Affairs.*

American Indian Authors for Young Readers

ABEITA, LOUISE, (E-YEH-SHURE'). Isleta Pueblo.

I am a Pueblo Indian Girl. William Morrow, 1939. 25 pp. Illus. by American Indian artists. Out of print. Grades 2-5.

E-Yeh-Shure' describes her way of life in her pueblo. She discusses such things as the making of bread in beehive ovens, hair washing with yucca plant roots, the types of clothes she wears, and hunting. Two of E-Yeh-Shure's poems are included. Beautifully illustrated.

ANAUTA, Eskimo
Children of the Blizzard, with Heluiz Chandler Washburne. Dennis Dobson, 1960. 192 pp. Illus. 75s. Grades 5 and up. Can be ordered through: British Book Center, Inc., 996 Lexington Ave., New York, N.Y. 10021

The author uses her own experiences as background for a series of interrelated stories about several Baffin Island Eskimo children. Different types of work—hunting, securing food, constructing shelter, making clothes—are described, as are friendships, relationships between adults and children, games and travel. A concluding chapter on games shows that they are not just for fun but are important for survival. A vocabulary of Eskimo words is included.

ANAUTA, Eskimo
Wild Like the Foxes: The True Story of an Eskimo Girl. John Daly, 1956. 192 pp. Grades 5 and up. Out of print.

This story is based on the life of the author's mother, Alea, and covers her girlhood up until she meets Yorgke, who becomes her husband. Hunting, trapping, playing boys' games, enduring hardships all are part of Alea's life until she is sent to school in England by her widowed father. Her return, her love for Yorgke, and the death of her father are described.

ANTELL, WILL, Chippewa
William Wipple Warren: Objibway Historian. Dillon Press, 1972. Approx. 50 pp. Illus. $3.95. Grades 5 and up.

This biography of William Whipple Warren, who was born in 1825, includes information on his family, work in the Territorial House of Representatives of which he was the only Indian member, his articles for a newspaper in St. Paul and his writing of a book about the Ojibways.

BENNETT, KAY, Navajo
Kaibah: Recollections of a Navajo Girlhood. Western Lore Press, 1964. Illus. by author. 253 pp. $7.50. Grades 8 and up.

Mrs. Bennett presents Navajos and Navajo family life as no outsider can. She writes of her years as a girl on the Navajo Reservation during the years 1928 to 1935. Her people are depicted with love and understanding.

BLACK ELK, Sioux.
Black Elk Speaks: Being the Life Story of a Holy Man of the Oglala Sioux, as told to John Neihardt. Univ. of Nebraska Press. 1961. 281 pp. Illus. by Standing Bear. $1.50 paperbound. Grades 10 and up.

Originally published in 1932, this is a personal narrative by one of the great spiritual leaders of the Oglala Sioux. Black Elk, a holy man who was born in 1863, gives a moving account of his life from early boyhood to the massacre at Wounded Knee in 1890 and the gathering of the Oglalas on the Pine Ridge Reservation in South Dakota.

BLACK HAWK, Sauk
Black Hawk: An Autobiography. Ed. by Donald Jackson. Peter Smith, 1955. 206 pp. Illus. $4.00 Univ. of Illinois Press. $1.75 paperbound. Grades 10 and up.

In the story of his life, recorded in 1833, seventy-year-old Black Hawk tells of his early battles with other tribes and ends with an account of his last flight from the United States Army and the merciless massacre of his people at Bad Axe, Wisconsin, in 1832.

BLUE EAGLE, ACEE, Pawnee-Creek
Echogee, the Little Blue Deer. Palmco Investment Corporation, Dallas, Texas, 1971. Illus. by author. 48 pages. $7.95 softcover with a sheet of transparent plastic for protection. Kindergarten - 3rd grade. Order from: Flagship Air Gifts, P.O. Box 5188, Church Street Station, New York, N.Y. 10049

Echogee (pronounced E-Joe-G), a little blue deer, bravely ventures away from his mother to explore the world. He encounters rabbits, skunks, turkeys and other animals who repeatedly caution him against straying too far. However, it is "dreadful noises" that finally send the little deer back to the comforting presence of his mother. There are twenty-two full color illustrations in this 9″ x 12″ book.

CHIEF JOSEPH, Nez Perce
Chief Joseph's Own Story, as told by Chief Joseph in 1879. Montana Reading Publications, 1972. Illus. with photographs. 31 pp. $1.25. Reading level: grade 3. Interest level: grades 6 to adult.

In this oration delivered in Washington, D.C., in 1879, Chief Joseph traces the history of Nez Perce contact with non-Indians beginning roughly in 1779, when French trappers traveled into eastern Oregon, to the time of his surrender, betrayal, and exile to Oklahoma Territory.

CLUTESI, GEORGE, Nootka.
Son of Raven, Son of Deer. Gray's Publishing Ltd., 1967. 126 pp. Illus. by author. $5.95. Grades 5 and up.

These twelve fables of the Tse-shaht people reveal various aspects of a rich culture. They are for teaching children the many wonders of nature, the importance of all living things, and to acquaint them with the closeness of man to all animals, birds and sea creatures. Good for reading aloud.

COHOE, WILLIAM, Cheyenne
A Cheyenne Sketchbook. Univ. of Oklahoma Press, 1964. 96 pp. Illus. by author. Out of Print. Grades 4 and up.

Cohoe, one of seventy-two warriors from the Great Plains taken as prisoners to Fort Marion, Florida, in 1875, sketched scenes from his past and from his life as a prisoner. The drawings are in three groups: life on the Plains, hunting; life on the Plains, ceremonies; life at Fort Marion, prisoners of war.

CRASHING THUNDER, Winnebago
Crashing Thunder: The Autobiography of a Winnebago. Ed. by Paul Radin. Dover, 1963, 91 pp. $1.25 paperbound. Grades 11 and up.

A re-publication of a 1920 edition, this life story of a Winnebago man incorporates a great deal of information about the tribe's customs. It is a forthright account of a boy's growing to manhood.

EASTMAN, CHARLES ALEXANDER (OHIYESA), Sioux.
Indian Boyhood. Dover Publications, 1971. 247 pp. Illus. $2.00 paperbound. Grades 5 and up.

Originally published in 1902, this is a first person account of the every-day happenings in the life of a young Santee Sioux boy. The time is immediately prior to the reservation period. Woven into the story are the customs, traditions, and religious beliefs of the tribe as they were then. The sentiments expressed in the first paragraph of the dedication are unworthy of the rest of the book.

EASTMAN, CHARLES ALEXANDER (OHIYESA), Sioux
Wigwam Evenings: Sioux Folk Tales Retold, with Elaine G. Eastman. Little, Brown, 1909. 352 pp. Illus. Out of print.

This collection of traditional Sioux stories is designed to be read or told to children of five and up.

FADDEN, RAY, Mohawk
Migration of the Iroquois. White Roots of Peace, 1972. Illus. 32 pp. 50¢ paperback. Order from: White Roots of Peace, Mohawk Nation at Akwesasne via Rooseveltown, N.Y. 13683.

This story is about the Hotinonsonni, or the People of the Longhouse, as recorded on a beaded belt which can be seen at the Six Nations Museum in Onchiota, N.Y.

FREDERICKS, OSWALD WHITE BEAR, Hopi
Book of the Hopi. Ed. by Frank Waters. Viking, 1963. 448 pp. Illus. by author. $12.50. Ballantine Books, $1.25 paperbound. Grades 9-12.

Drawings, and source material recorded by Mr. Fredericks are the heart of this account of Hopi history, religion, customs and ceremonies. Thirty members of the tribe tell of their experiences and of their efforts to maintain their spiritual beliefs.

FREUCHEN, PIPALUK, Eskimo
Eskimo Boy. Lothrop, Lee, 1951. 96 pp. Illus. $3.95. Grades 3 and up.

Ivik pledges to take on the job of finding food for his family after his father is killed in a hunting accident. Bad luck and inexperience finally force the young boy to undertake a long and hazardous journey across the ice to seek help on the mainland. The story of Ivik's long trek, his encounter with a polar bear, eventual rescue and triumphant return is told with unrelenting realism.

GERONIMO, Apache.
Geronimo: His Own Story. Ed. by Steven Melvil Barrett. E. P. Dutton, 1970. 190 pp. Illus. $7.95. Ballantine Books, $1.25 paperbound.

In this story of his life, dictated while he was imprisoned at Fort Sill, Oklahoma Territory, Geronimo gives both a cultural and an historical account of the Apaches.

JOSIE, EDITH, Loucheaux.
Here are the News. Clark, Irwin, 1966. 135 pp. Illus. with photographs. $3.95. Grades 7 and up.

This book contains the newspaper columns of Edith Josie which have appeared in the *Whitehorse Star* since the fall of 1962. She writes of the Indian village of Old Crow located on the banks of the Porcupine River inside the Arctic Circle. Her accounts of trapping, fishing, incoming planes, and dogsled races reflect what is considered newsworthy in Old Crow. The articles also record a way of life that is gradually being changed by contact with the outside world.

LaFLESCHE, FRANCIS, Omaha
The Middle Five: Indian Schoolboys of the Omaha Tribe. Univ. of Wisconsin Press, 1963. 152 pp. Illus. $2.50 paperbound. Grades 4 and up.

This reprint of a 1900 edition describes LaFlesche's experiences at the Presbyterian Mission School in Bellevue, Nebraska, during the 1860's.

LaPOINTE, FRANK, Sioux
The Sioux Today. Macmillan Company, 1972. 144 pp. Illus. $4.95. Grades 7 and up.

Vignettes of the lives of Sioux people today, based on the author's own reservation experience, tell about Chuck, who decides to let his hair grow and is called a "militant"; Louis, who does not want to admit to being a Sioux; Shirley, who at fourteen serves as mother to five; and Betty, a "new Indian" who refuses to be called a "squaw." Excellent.

LYONS, OREN, Onondaga
Dog Story. Holiday House, 1973. 32 pp. Illus. by author. $3.95. Kindergarten-grade 1.

Mr. Lyons writes of his boyhood on the Onondaga Reservation in upstate New York and of his dog Smudgie. This is a touching story of how a boy and dog meet and of the deep friendship that develops between them.

MARKOOSIE, Eskimo
Harpoon of the Hunter. McGill-Queen's Univ. Press, 1970. 81 pp. Illus. by Germaine Arnaktauyok. $4.95. Grades 7 and up.

The hero of this story, young Kamik, tracks down a wounded polar bear and makes a long journey home alone after his companions have been killed. Life in the Canadian Arctic is depicted as an unrelenting, brutal, often fatal, struggle for survival.

MAYOKOK, ROBERT, Eskimo
Mr. Mayokok, a well-known artist, has written and illustrated five paperbound booklets:

The Alaskan Eskimo (11 pp.) contains information on Eskimo food, Native clothing, hunting and fishing. 50¢

Eskimo Customs (36 pp.) tells of such customs as piercing lips and tatooing and also has information on the Eskimo language. $1.50

Eskimo Life (21 pp.) tells about oogrook, hunting, catching birds and arctic hare. $1.50

Eskimo Stories (42 pp.) is a selection of traditional tales. $1.50

True Eskimo Stories (36 pp.) tells about the hair seal, seal hunting, how the seal is used, dog teams, walrus and driftwood. $1.00

Order from: Mr. Robert Mayokok, 1406 Twining Avenue, Anchorage, Alaska 99504 (Payment must accompany order.)

McGAA, ED, Sioux
Red Cloud: The Story of an American Indian.
Dillon Press, 1971. 54 pp. Illus. with photographs.
$3.95. Grades 8 and up.

Red Cloud, an Oglala Sioux, struggled during the second half of the nineteenth century to save his people from cultural and physical destruction. This great leader emerges as a vigorous man whose incisive mind enables him to state his case with sharp wit and sly humor. Written by a member of the Oglala Sioux Tribe, this biography contains information about Sioux culture.

McNICKLE, D'ARCY, Flathead
Indian Tribes of the United States: Ethnic and Cultural Survival. Oxford Univ. Press, 1962. 79 pp.
$1.75 paperbound. Grades 8 and up.

A discussion of American Indian attempts to adjust to Anglo-American culture and why the efforts have failed.

McNICKLE, D'ARCY, Flathead
Runner in the Sun: A Story of Indian Maize. Holt, Rinehart, Winston, 1954. 234 pp. Illus. by Allan Houser. $3.27. Grades 7 and up.

An adventure story as well as the history of a town settled centuries before Columbus set sail from Spain, this novel is a scholarly reconstruction of the life, customs and beliefs of the ancient cliff-dwelling settlements of the southwestern United States. Salt, a teenage boy, is chosen to make a hazardous journey to Mexico in search of a hardier strain of corn and a better life for the people of his village.

MONTURE, ETHEL BRANT, Mohawk
Famous Indians: Canadian Portraits. Clarke, Irwin, 1960. 160 pp. $3.50. Grades 10 and up.

The life stories of Joseph Brant (1742-1806), a Mohawk, Crowfoot (1821-1889), a Blackfeet, and Oronhyatekha (1841-1907), a Mohawk, are set against the background of their times. These concisely written biographies contain a great deal of historical and cultural information.

MOUNTAIN WOLF WOMAN, Winnebago
Mountain Wolf Woman: Sister of Crashing Thunder. Ed. by Nancy Oestreich Lurie. Univ. of Michigan Press, 1961. 142 pp. $4.95. $1.95 paperbound. Grades 10 and up.

An unusually candid and authentic account of Indian life—told from a woman's point of view. In this narrative, recorded on tape and then translated into English, Mountain Wolf Woman at the age of seventy-five describes her wandering childhood days in Wisconsin, her brief stay at a mission school, the marriage arranged against her will, the death of her chosen husband and the misfortunes of her children.

NEZ PERCE TRIBE
Ne Mee Poom Tit Wah Tit (Nez Perce Legends). Nez Perce Tribe, 1972. 214 pp. Illus. by Leroy L. Seth. $12.50 plus 50¢ handling. Grades 7 and up.

Coyote, the principal character in these legends, is known as a trickster-transformer. Sometimes a man, sometimes an animal, he possesses supernatural powers and can change himself, other animals, people and objects in various ways. He is a silly, clumsy, stupid, laughable rascal who gets into one scrape after another but he is also a cheerful, happy creature who is in no way evil. By acting out man's socially disruptive drives, the trickster (Coyote) reveals in these stories the results of violating conventional Nez Perce mores. Stories of Coyote's exploits are used to teach Nez Perce children how to behave properly and to instill in a child values which will help him become a good person. This book, sponsored and edited by the Nez Perce Tribe, is the first of a three-phase project on the history and culture of the Nez Perce Tribe. Good for reading-telling.

NULIGAK, Eskimo
I, Nuligak. Translated from the Eskimo by Maurice Metayer. Peter Martin, 1968. 208 pp. $5.95. Pocket Books, $1.25 paperbound. Grades 7 and up.

This autobiography of a member of the Kitigariukmeut tribe of Canadian Eskimos spans the years from 1895 to 1966. It is simply told and reveals the gaiety, laughter and warmth of Eskimo community life as well as the physical hardship and privations of life in the harsh Arctic environment.

PARKER, ARTHUR C., Seneca
Skunny Wundy: Seneca Indian Tales. Albert Whitman and Co., 1970. 224 pp. $3.95. Grades 5 and up.

Different animals take on different traits in these tales: Fox and Raccoon are clever, while Rabbit is often easily fooled; Bear is brave but not very smart, and Wolf is frequently a villain. Originally published in 1926, these stories are good for reading aloud.

PLENTY-COUPS, Crow.
Plenty-Coups, Chief of the Crows. Ed. by Frank Bird Linderman. Univ. of Nebraska Press, 1962. 324 pp. $1.50 paperbound. Grades 10 and up.

Eighty-year-old Chief Plenty-Coups discusses his boyhood, how he became a chief, and describes his participation in the tribal customs of the Crow Indians. This book was originally published in 1930 as *American, The Life Story of a Great Indian, Plenty-Coups, Chief of the Crows.*

SENUNGETUK, JOSEPH E., Eskimo
Give or Take a Century: An Eskimo Chronicle. The Indian Historian Press, 1970. 120 pp. Illus. by author. $12.00. Grades 10 and up.

The author tells the history of an Eskimo family (his) in Alaska as they move from a century filled with the customs, traditions, and lifeways of an ancient time into a new century in which they are confronted and confused by the mores, social life, and technology of a different culture.

SHAW, ANNA MOORE, Pima
Pima Indian Legends. Univ. of Arizona Press, 1968. 111 pp. $2.50 paperbound. Grades 6 and up.

Mrs. Shaw relates stories heard from her parents and grandparents, and combines ancient Pima history with more current happenings.

SILOOK, ROGER, Eskimo
. . . . . *In the Beginning.* Helen A. White. 1970 Approx. 20 pp. Illus. by Robert Mayokok. $2.85 plus postage. Paperbound. Grades 6 and up.

This is the story of Eskimos in pre-historic Alaska as told by two Alaskan Eskimos in simple words and drawings. Order from: Helen A. White, 7323 Duben Ave., Anchorage, Alaska 99504. It will be a surprise to some to learn that Alaska was once "warm all three hundred and sixty-five days a year."

SNEVE, VIRGINIA DRIVING HAWK, Sioux
High Elk's Treasure. Holiday House, 1972. 96 pp.
Illus. by Oren Lyons. $4.95. Grades 3-6.

This story about the William High Elk family, a contemporary Sioux family, has many dimensions. It is an adventure story with an element of mystery regarding the contents of an old rawhide bundle discovered in a cave where young Joe High Elk takes refuge from a storm. It is also a story about Sioux life on a Plains Indian reservation.

SNEVE, VIRGINIA DRIVING HAWK, Sioux
Jimmy Yellow Hawk. Holiday House, 1972. 76 pp.
Illus. by Oren Lyons. $4.50. Grades 3-6.

This story about a contemporary Sioux boy living on an Indian reservation in South Dakota tells of the excitement of a rodeo, a search for a lost mare in a dangerous storm, the pageantry of a tribal dance contest, and learning to trap animals properly.

STANDS IN TIMBER, JOHN, Northern
Cheyenne

Cheyenne Memories. Yale Univ. Press, 1967. 330
pp. Illus. $10.00. Univ. of Nebraska Press, $2.25
paperbound. Grades 11 and up.

Mr. Stands In Timber offers a record of Cheyenne life from legendary times to life on the Northern Cheyenne Reservation in Montana.

TALL BULL, HENRY, Cheyenne
Cheyenne Fire Fighters. Montana Reading Publications, 1971. Illus. with photographs. 39 pp. $1.00
paperbound. Reading level: grade 4. Interest level:
grade 4 to adult.

This is about a crew of Cheyenne men who fight forest fires. The story opens with the sighting of smoke on the horizon by a forest ranger, describes how forest fires behave, and details modern methods used to contain and control forest fires.

TALL BULL, HENRY, Cheyenne
Grandfather and the Popping Machine. Montana
Reading Publications, 1970, 32 pp. $1.00. Reading
level: grade 3. Interest level: grades 4-8.

Humorous stories current among the Northern Cheyennes.

TALL BULL, HENRY, Cheyenne
The Spotted Horse. Montana Reading Publications, 1970. 33 pp. $1.00. Reading level: grade 3. Interest level: grades 4-8.

Little Thunder breaks in his first horse, saves the camp's horse herd, and participates in a buffalo hunt.

TALL BULL, HENRY, Cheyenne
The Winter Hunt. Montana Reading Publications, 1971. 32 pp. $1.00. Reading level: grade 5. Interest level: grades 5-8.

In the first story Little Thunder and Spotted Horse search for badly-needed food. In "Snake Medicine," Little Fawn is bitten by a rattlesnake while she and her mother are picking Juneberries. Black Hair treats the bite and saves her life. In the third story, two women, Good Feather and Red Tassel, make it possible for the men of the camp to capture seven horses.

TOINEETA, JOY YELLOWTAIL, Crow
Indian Tales of the Northern Plains, with Sally Old Coyote. Montana Reading Publications, 1972. Illus. 32 pp. $1.25. Reading level: grade 3. Interest level: grades 2-4.

The authors present a rich collection of Blackfeet, Sioux, Cheyenne, Crow, Flathead and Arapahoe "how and why" stories.

TOINEETA, JOY YELLOWTAIL, Crow
Indian Tales of the Northern Rockies, with Sally Old Coyote. Montana Reading Publications, 1972. Illus. 32 pp. $1.00. Reading level: grade 2. Interest level: grades 1-4.

This volume recounts folk tales from the Blackfeet, Flathead, Gros Ventre, Nez Perce and Shoshone tribes.

TWO LEGGINGS, Crow
Two Leggings: The Making of a Crow Warrior. Ed. by Peter Nabokov. Crowell, 1967. 226 pp. Hardbound edition out of print. Apollo Editions, Inc. $2.95 paperbound. Grades 10 and up.

This is a first-person account of the everyday life of a nineteenth-century Crow Indian man. Two Leggings describes the process of becoming a Crow warrior and gives a great deal of information on the religious and social values of a Plains Indian people.

VELARDE, PABLITA, Santa Clara Pueblo
Old Father, The Story Teller. Dale Stuart King, 1960. 66 pp. Illus. by author. Out of print. Grades 7 and up.

A Tewa artist writes the stories and legends she heard from her grandfather and great-grandfather.

WEBB, GEORGE, Pima
A Pima Remembers. Univ. of Arizona Press, 1959. 126 pp. Illus. $3.00. Grades 7 and up.

Mr. Webb wrote this book to acquaint young Pimas with some of the background and traditions of their own people. He describes in short-story form the old ways, a rabbit hunt, Pima games, his own school days, a horse round-up, and includes some Pima legends. He describes Pima life before and after a dam was built across the Gila River upstream of the Pimas.

WELCH, JAMES, Blackfeet
Riding the Earthboy 40. World, 1971. 54 pp. $6.95. Grades 9 and up.

These forty-six poems, rich in the imagery of the land and Indian life, are moving comments on the human experience and one man's search for meaning in a difficult world. His first collection of poems, *Earthboy* immediately establishes Mr. Welch in the forefront of younger American poets.

WOODEN LEG, Cheyenne
Wooden Leg: A Warrior Who Fought Custer, as told to Thomas B. Marquis. Univ. of Nebraska Press, 1962. 389 pp. $2.25 paperbound. Grades 10 and up.

This reprint of a 1931 edition is the narrative of a Cheyenne warrior who fought against Custer at the Battle of the Little Big Horn. It includes observations on Cheyenne daily life and tribal customs.

YELLOW ROBE, ROSEBUD (LACOTAWIN), Sioux

An Album of the American Indian. Franklin Watts, Inc., 1969. 96 pp. Illus. $4.95. Grades 5 and up.

Paintings, drawings, and photographs, accompanied by a brief text, serve to illustrate various facets of American Indian cultures and history from past to present. Although designed primarily for young adults, this album will be of interest to all ages.

ZUNI PUEBLO
The Zunis: Self-Portrayals, by the Zuni People. Translated by Alvina Quam. Univ. of New Mexico Press, 1972. 245 pp. Photographs. $7.95 hardcover. $3.95 paperbound. Grades 6 and up.

Here for the first time in print are forty-six stories from the great oral literature of the Zunis of New Mexico. The creation story, rituals of masked dances, farming and hunting practices, battles, fables and history are all recorded in this book. There are tales of ghosts and personified animals, as well as fables told to discipline children or to warn them against foolhardy bravery and bragadoccio. Some of the stories are simply for entertainment and some deal directly with the problems of modern society. In his introduction, Robert E. Lewis, Governor of the Pueblo, says, "We are proud to present this, the first volume of stories told by the oldest members of my Zuni people, for your reading enjoyment—the old and young, in classroom or home."

MISCELLANEOUS

BALLARD, LOUIS W. Cherokee-Quapaw
American Indian Music for the Class Room. Canyon Records, 1973. Recording plus teaching package: $39.50 LP. $44.50 tape cassette. Order from: Canyon Records, 4143 North Sixteenth Street, Phoenix, Arizona 85016. All grades.

This music-education package presents American Indian music for classroom study and performance. Song analyses and dance diagrams are provided. The package includes music and dances representing thirty-five tribes along with cultural information on over fifty North American Indian tribes, plus Eskimos. A valuable teaching tool for music classes as well as for general study, sociology, ethnic studies, etc.

Eskimo Cook Book. Easter Seal Society for Alaska Crippled Children and Adults, 1952. 36 pp. 50¢—60¢ postpaid, paperbound.

The students at Shishmaref Day School in Shishmaref, Alaska, supplied these recipes. Included are dishes such as salted duck, bear paws, salmon berries, walrus stew and Eskimo ice cream. This booklet presents a child's eye view of cooking. Some of the recipes include a description of how to obtain the food and prepare it. The cooking instructions often consist of "Put them in a pot to boil. Add salt and water." Order from Easter Seal Society for Alaska Crippled Children and Adults, P.O. Box 2432, Anchorage, Alaska. 99510

Photographs and Poems by Sioux Children. Tipi Shop, Inc., 1971. 80 pp. $2.50. Grades 6 and up.

Thirteen teenage students of the Porcupine Day School on the Pine Ridge Reservation in South Dakota took the photographs presented in this exhibition catalog. The pictures are accompanied by poems written by the student photographers and their classmates. The photographs explore many aspects of life and the natural environment of the Porcupine community and document western rural life during the winter season of 1969-70. The poems are an extension of the photographic themes. Order from: Tipi Shop, Inc., P.O. Box 1270, Rapid City, S. D. 57701.

Tales from the Longhouse. Gray's Publishing Ltd., 1973. 112 pp. $4.95. Grades 6 and up.

Indian students living on Vancouver Island and in the village of Kingcome Inlet on the British Columbia coast gathered these stories and legends from older relatives over a six-year period. The stories are from the various Indian bands in British Columbia and are arranged under such headings as origins, power, nature, crafts, customs, animals, birds and legends.

Tales of Eskimo Alaska. Alaska Methodist University Press, 1971. 91 pp. Illus. $4.50. All grades.

This collection of tales and legends from four areas of Alaska includes legends of the supernatural, a story about mischievous children, a porcupine hunt, a tale of Eskimo war and stories about the mythic past.

The Weewish Tree, a magazine of Indian America for young people. The Indian Historian Press. Published six times a year during the school year. One year: $6.50. Two years: $11.00. Three years: $17.00. Discounts available for bulk orders. Grades 1 through high school.

Written and illustrated by American Indians, young and old, this magazine contains stories, poetry, games, history, myths, legends, illustrations, and cultural articles written for young people.

The Whispering Winds: Poetry by Young American Indians. Ed. by Terry Allen. Doubleday, 1972. $1.95 paperbound. Grades 8 and up.

A collection of poems written by students at the Institute of American Indian Arts in Santa Fe., N. M., a combined academic high school and art institute. The poetry covers such varied themes as Indian lore, the Vietnam War, childhood memories, thirst and loneliness. A brief biography of each poet precedes his or her poems.

List of Publishers

Alaska Methodist Univ. Press
Wesley Drive
Anchorage, Alaska 99504

Apollo Editions, Inc.
201 Park Ave. S.
New York, N.Y. 10003

Ballantine & Co.
101 Fifth Ave.
New York, N.Y. 10003

Black Hills Books
511 St. Joe Street
Rapid City, S.D. 58701

Childrens Press
1224 West Van Buren St.
Chicago, Ill. 60607

Clark, Irwin and Co., Ltd.
Clarwin House
791 St. Clair Ave., W.
Toronto 10
Ontario, Can.

Thomas Y. Crowell
201 Park Ave. South
New York, N.Y. 10003

Dakota Press
University of South Dakota
Vermillion, S.D. 57069

Dillon Press
106 Washington Ave. N.
Minneapolis, Minn. 55401

Doubleday & Co. Inc.
277 Park Ave.
New York, N.Y. 10017

Dover Publications, Inc.
180 Varick St.
New York, N.Y. 10014

E. P. Dutton & Co., Inc.
201 Park Ave. S.
New York, N.Y. 10003

Easter Seal Society of Alaska
Crippled Children & Adults
P.O. Box 2432
Anchorage, Alaska

M. Evans & Co., Inc.
216 E. 49 St.
New York, N.Y. 10017

Golden Bell Press
2400 Curtis St.
Denver, Colo. 80205

Gray's Publishing Ltd.
Box 718
Sidney, B.C.
Canada

Holiday House
18 E. 56 St.
New York, N.Y. 10022

Holt, Rinehart & Winston, Inc.
383 Madison Ave.
New York, N.Y. 10017

The Indian Historian Press
1451 Masonic Ave.
San Francisco, Cal. 94117

Lothrop, Lee & Shepard, Co.
105 Madison Ave.
New York, N.Y. 10016

The Macmillan Co.
866 Third Ave.
New York, N.Y. 10022

McGill-Queen's Univ. Press
3458 Redpath St.
Montreal 109, P.Q.
Canada

Montana Reading Publications
Level 4
Stapleton Bldg.
Billings, Mont. 59101

Nez Perce Tribe
Box 305
Lapwai, Idaho 83540

Oxford University Press, Inc.
200 Madison Ave.
New York, N.Y. 10016

Pocket Books
630 Fifth Ave.
New York, N.Y. 10020

Tipi Shop, Inc.
P.O. Box 1270
Rapid City, S.D. 57701

Univ. of Arizona Press
Box 3398
Tucson, Ariz. 85722

Univ. of Illinois Press
Urbana
Illinois 61901

The Univ. of Michigan Press
Ann Arbor
Michigan 48106

Univ. of Nebraska Press
901 N. 17 St.
Lincoln, Neb. 68508

Univ. of New Mexico Press
Albuquerque
New Mexico 87106

Univ. of Oklahoma Press
1005 Asp Ave.
Norman, Okla. 73069

Univ. of Wisconsin Press
Box 1379
Madison, Wisc. 53701

The Viking Press, Inc.
625 Madison Ave.
New York, N.Y. 10002

Franklin Watts, Inc.
845 Third Ave.
New York, N.Y. 10022

Westernlore Press
Box 41073, E. R. Sta.
Los Angeles, Calif. 90041

Albert Whitman & Co.
560 W. Lake St.
Chicago, Ill. 60606

World Publishing Co.
110 E. 59 St.
New York, N.Y. 10022

Yale University Press
149 York St.
New Haven, Conn. 06511